# BOOKER T. WASHINGTON

by Jehan Jones-Radgowski

PEBBLE
a capstone imprint

Pebble Explore is published by Pebble, an imprint of Capstone.
1710 Roe Crest Drive, North Mankato, Minnesota 56003
www.capstonepub.com

**Library of Congress Cataloging-in-Publication data is available
on the Library of Congress website.**
ISBN: 978-1-9771-1361-0 (library binding)
ISBN: 978-1-9771-1805-9 (paperback)
ISBN: 978-1-9771-1369-6 (eBook PDF)

Summary: Explores the life, challenges, and accomplishments of
educator and author Booker T. Washington.

**Image Credits**
Alamy: ClassicStock, 12; Library of Congress: cover, 1, 5, 16, 19, 22, 23, 25,
26, 29, Photographs in the Carol M. Highsmith Archive, 6, 7, 27; North Wind
Picture Archives: 8, 11, 18; Shutterstock: Everett Historical, 21, kapooklook01
(geometric background), cover, back cover, 2, 29, Weredragon, 15

**Editorial Credits**
Erika L. Shores, editor; Elyse White, designer; Svetlana Zhurkin,
media researcher; Katy LaVigne, production specialist

All internet sites appearing in back matter were available and accurate when
this book was sent to press.

Printed and bound in China.
2489

# Table of Contents

Words in **bold** are in the glossary.

# Who Was Booker T. Washington?

Booker T. Washington was a teacher. He wrote books and **speeches**. He led a school for black people about 140 years ago.

Booker spoke out for black people in the United States. He wanted white people to know about their lives. When Booker was a child, many black people were **enslaved**. They were made to work with no pay. They could not go to school. Even after the **law** made them free, black people were treated unfairly by white people.

# Childhood

Booker was born in 1856 in Virginia. His mother named him Booker Taliaferro. He gave himself the last name Washington at age 10.

The cabin where Booker lived in Virginia

Inside Booker's childhood cabin

Booker's mother was a cook on a big farm. As an enslaved person, she was made to live and work there. Booker's house was tiny. He slept on the floor. His bed was a pile of rags. In summer the house was very hot. During winter it was always cold.

Enslaved children were forced to work.

As an enslaved child, Booker had
to work. He moved big sacks of corn
to a mill every week. The mill was
3 miles (4.8 kilometers) away.

One day Booker carried the
schoolbooks of the farm owner's
daughter. He wondered what school
was like. Booker badly wanted to
find out.

In 1860, Booker's mother married Washington Ferguson. In 1865, a law was passed. No one could be enslaved anymore. Booker and his family were free. They moved to Malden, West Virginia.

Booker's stepfather found him a job. Booker was about 9 years old. He worked in a salt **mine**. It was hard work moving and packing salt. Booker dreamed of learning to read.

The inside of a building where salt was made

After slavery ended, black children were finally allowed to go to school.

Booker's parents said he could go to school. But he had to get his work done first. To do this, Booker started work at 4:00 in the morning.

Soon Booker got a new job. He cleaned the house of Viola Ruffner. She had been a teacher. She and Booker became friends. She helped him learn and go to school.

Booker gave some of his money to his family. He saved the rest. It would help him with his dream. He wanted to go to **college**.

In 1872, Booker was 16 years old. He set out for Hampton, Virginia. It was 500 miles (805 km) away from where Booker lived in Malden, West Virginia. He wanted to go to the Hampton **Institute**. It was a college for black students. Would he be let into the school? Would he have enough money for his trip and school?

Booker did not give up on his way to Hampton. He ran out of money many times. He stopped and found jobs. In one town, Booker worked taking goods off ships.

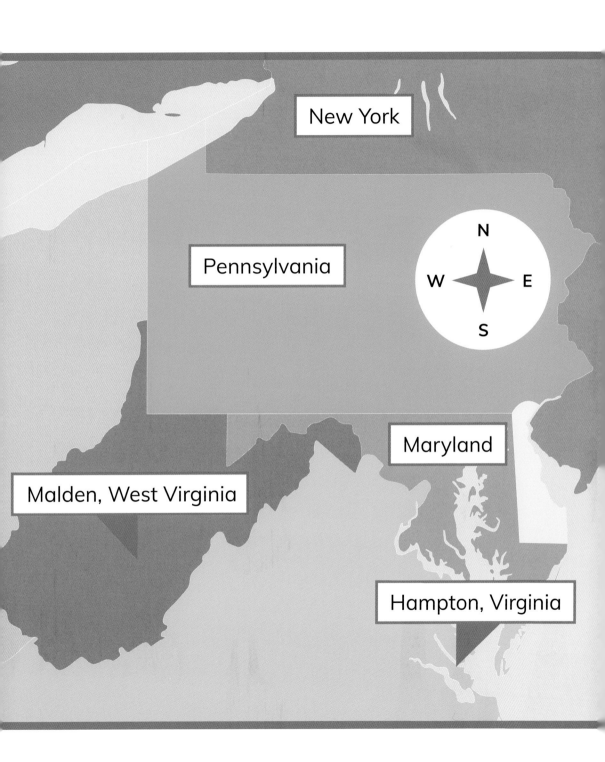

New York

Pennsylvania

Maryland

Malden, West Virginia

Hampton, Virginia

N
W E
S

Hampton Institute in 1899

At last, Booker made it to Hampton. He had only 50 cents left. He took a job cleaning the school. He made money so he could take classes. Booker did well at Hampton. He became very good at speaking in front of people.

Booker was done with school after three years. He was 19. He went back home. He worked as a teacher. He wanted every child to go to school and learn to read.

# Life's Work

In 1879, Booker gave a speech at Hampton Institute. Two weeks later, the school gave him a job. In 1881, Booker left and started a new school. It was in Tuskegee, Alabama.

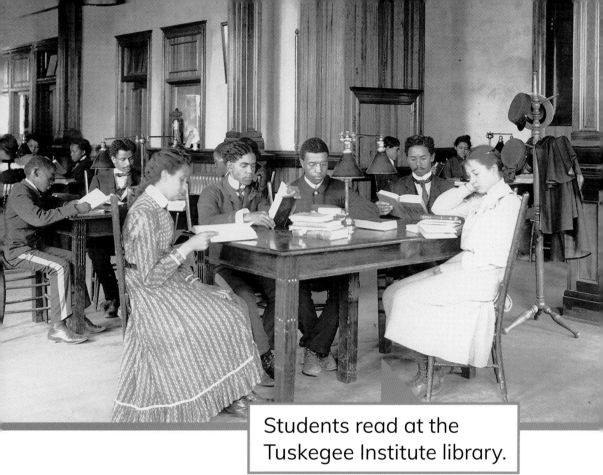

Students read at the Tuskegee Institute library.

Many black people wanted to go to Booker's school. He said he would help them change their lives. Booker's school was called the Tuskegee Institute. It helped black people learn to be good farmers and teachers.

Booker's school grew. More people were hearing about him. In 1895, Booker gave a speech about how black and white people could get along in the future. It was the first time a black man spoke to a group of both white and black people.

Booker spoke and wrote about his life and ideas. One book was read by many people. The book was called *Up from Slavery*. It came out in 1901. That same year, Booker met President Theodore Roosevelt. Booker was the first black person to eat dinner with a president at the White House.

Booker and
Theodore Roosevelt

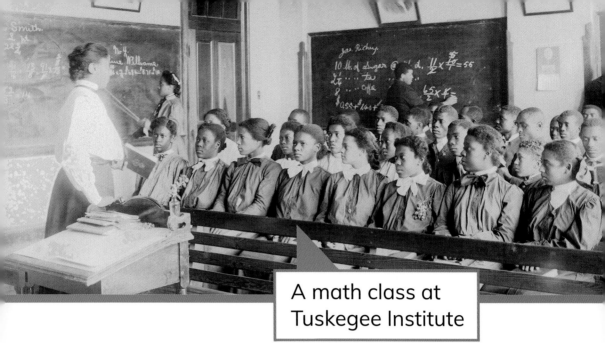

A math class at Tuskegee Institute

Not everyone liked Booker. Some black leaders thought it was most important that everyone be treated the same. Booker said it was better for black people to go to school and become good farmers and teachers. Booker said the fight to be treated **equal** would not be safe. He said they should take more time to gain better treatment.

Booker's ideas made some black people mad. But most felt the same about one thing. They all knew going to school was important.

A science class at Tuskegee Institute

# Later Years

   Booker married three times.
His first wife was Fanny Norton Smith.
They had a daughter named Portia
in 1883. Fanny died a year later.

   In 1886, Booker married Olivia
Davidson. She was a teacher. She
helped run the Tuskegee Institute with
Booker. They had two sons, Booker Jr.
and Ernest. Olivia died in 1889.

   Booker married Margaret Murray
in 1902. She also worked at Tuskegee.
She helped care for Booker's children.
She lived until 1925.

Booker with his wife, Margaret, and sons in 1906

Booker worked very hard even as he got older. He spoke at places all over the country. He also still led the Tuskegee Institute. Even if he was sick, Booker kept working to help black people. On November 14, 1915, Booker died. He was 59.

Today people still remember Booker's work. Parks, schools, and ships have been named after him.

Booker T. Washington statue at Tuskegee University

# Important Dates

**1856** — Booker T. Washington is born in 1856 in Franklin County, Virginia.

**1861** — The U.S. Civil War begins.

**1865** — The Civil War ends. People can no longer own slaves in the United States.

**1872** — Booker leaves West Virginia for Hampton Institute in Hampton, Virginia.

**1875** — Booker finishes his schooling at the Hampton Institute.

**1881** — Booker starts a new school called the Tuskegee Institute in Alabama.

**1895** — Booker gives a speech. It is later called the Atlanta Compromise.

**1901** — Booker's book, *Up from Slavery*, comes out. Booker goes to the White House to have dinner with President Theodore Roosevelt.

**1915** — Booker dies at age 59.

# Fast Facts

**Name:**
Booker T. Washington

**Role:**
teacher, author, speaker

**Life dates:**
April 5, 1856 to November 14, 1915

**Key accomplishments:**
Booker T. Washington was the leader of the Tuskegee Institute. He wrote about his life in the book *Up from Slavery*.

# Glossary

**college** (KOL-ij)—a place of higher learning where students can study after they finish high school

**enslave** (in-SLAYV)—to make someone lose their freedom

**equal** (EE-kwul)—being the same

**institute** (IN-stuh-toot)—a school that is set up for a special purpose

**law** (LAW)—a rule made by a government that must be followed

**mine** (MINE)—a place where workers dig up minerals that are underground

**speech** (SPEECH)—a talk given to a group of people

# Read More

Buckley Jr., James. *Who Was Booker T. Washington?* New York : Penguin Workshop, 2018.

Haldy, Emma E. *Booker T. Washington.* My Itty-Bitty Bio. Ann Arbor, MI: Cherry Lake Publishing, 2017.

Harrison, Vashti. *Little Legends: Exceptional Men in Black.* New York: Little, Brown and Company, 2019.

# Internet Sites

*Booker T. Washingtion National Monument* https://www.nps.gov/bowa/index.htm

*Tuskegee University: Booker T. Washington* https://www.tuskegee.edu/discover-tu/tu-presidents/booker-t-washington

# Index